ATTRACTING CUSTOMERS 101

CONTENTS

INTRODUCTION

Attracting customers is a vital aspect of any business strategy, as it lays the foundation for growth, profitability, and long-term success. In today's competitive market, capturing the attention of potential customers requires a thoughtful and well-executed approach. There are several key strategies that can help businesses effectively attract customers and build a loyal customer base.

Firstly, understanding the target audience is essential. Conducting market research and analyzing customer demographics, preferences, and behaviors can provide valuable insights to tailor marketing efforts accordingly. Utilizing this information, businesses can develop compelling value propositions that resonate with their target customers.

Secondly, a strong online presence is crucial. Creating an engaging website, optimizing it for search engines, and utilizing social media platforms effectively can significantly enhance visibility and attract customers. By consistently providing valuable and relevant content, interacting with customers, and actively managing online reviews, businesses can establish credibility and attract new customers.

Moreover, implementing targeted marketing campaigns through various channels such as email marketing, pay-per-click advertising, and influencer partnerships can be highly effective in reaching and attracting customers. Offering incentives like discounts, promotions, or loyalty programs can also entice customers to choose a particular brand over competitors.

Overall, attracting customers requires a multi-faceted approach that combines market research, online presence, targeted marketing, and customer engagement. By understanding their target audience and implementing effective strategies, businesses can successfully attract customers and foster lasting relationships.

Step 1
Define Your Target Audience and Unique Selling Proposition

Attracting customers begins with a clear understanding of your target audience and a compelling unique selling proposition (USP) that sets your business apart from competitors. Identifying and defining your target audience helps you tailor your marketing efforts to reach the right people who are most likely to be interested in your products or services.

Start by conducting market research to gather insights about your potential customers. Explore factors such as demographics, psychographics, purchasing behaviors, and preferences. This information will help you create buyer personas that represent your ideal customers and guide your marketing strategies.

Once you have a solid grasp of your target audience, it's crucial to develop a unique selling proposition. Your USP is what differentiates your business from others and showcases the value you offer. It could be a specific feature, exceptional customer service, competitive pricing, or a combination of factors that make your business stand out.

To create an effective USP, consider the needs and pain points of your target audience and how your products or services address those issues better than your competitors. Craft a compelling and concise statement that clearly communicates your unique value proposition and resonates with your target customers.

By defining your target audience and developing a strong USP, you lay the foundation for attracting customers who are genuinely interested in what your business has to offer. These crucial initial steps will guide your marketing efforts and ensure that you are effectively reaching the right people with a compelling message.

Step 2
Enhance Your Online Presence

In today's digital age, a strong online presence is paramount for attracting customers. It serves as a virtual storefront where potential customers can discover and engage with your business. Enhancing your online presence involves optimizing your website, utilizing social media platforms, and implementing effective digital marketing strategies.

Start by ensuring that your website is visually appealing, user-friendly, and optimized for search engines. Optimize your website's content with relevant keywords to improve its visibility in search engine results. Provide valuable and informative content that showcases your expertise and addresses the needs of your target audience.

In addition to your website, leverage the power of social media platforms to engage with your audience and attract customers. Identify the platforms that your target audience frequents the most and create compelling profiles that reflect your brand's identity. Regularly share engaging content, interact with your followers, and respond promptly to their inquiries and feedback.

Implementing digital marketing strategies such as search engine optimization (SEO), pay-per-click (PPC) advertising, email marketing, and content marketing can also significantly enhance your online presence and attract customers. Tailor your marketing campaigns to reach your target audience effectively and utilize analytics to measure the success of your efforts.

Furthermore, actively managing your online reputation is crucial. Encourage satisfied customers to leave positive reviews and promptly address any negative feedback or complaints. A positive online reputation builds trust and credibility, which can attract new customers.

By enhancing your online presence, you increase your visibility, credibility, and accessibility to potential customers. It creates opportunities for engagement, fosters brand awareness, and ultimately helps attract customers to your business.

Step 3
Implement Targeted Marketing Campaigns

To attract customers effectively, it's essential to implement targeted marketing campaigns that reach your intended audience with the right message at the right time. By understanding your target audience's preferences and behaviors, you can tailor your marketing efforts to resonate with them and drive customer engagement.

Email marketing is a powerful tool for reaching potential customers directly. Build an email list by offering incentives like exclusive discounts or valuable content in exchange for email subscriptions. Segment your email list based on demographics or past purchase history to send personalized and relevant messages that cater to the specific needs and interests of different customer segments.

Pay-per-click (PPC) advertising is another effective strategy for attracting customers. Utilize platforms like Google Ads or social media advertising to display targeted ads to users searching for relevant keywords or demographics that align with your target audience. Craft compelling ad copy and optimize landing pages to encourage click-throughs and conversions.

Collaborating with influencers in your industry can also help attract customers. Identify influencers whose audience aligns with your target market and engage them in partnerships or sponsored content. Influencers can promote your products or services to their followers, leveraging their trust and influence to drive customer interest and generate conversions.

Furthermore, consider running promotions, discounts, or loyalty programs to incentivize customers to choose your business over competitors. Offering exclusive deals or rewards for repeat purchases can create a sense of urgency and build customer loyalty.

Regularly analyze the performance of your marketing campaigns, track key metrics, and make data-driven adjustments to optimize your efforts. Continuously refine your targeting, messaging, and channels based on customer feedback and market trends to ensure the effectiveness of your marketing strategies.

By implementing targeted marketing campaigns, you can effectively reach and engage with your target audience, driving customer interest and conversions. These focused efforts increase the likelihood of attracting customers who are more likely to convert into loyal patrons of your business.

Step 4
Provide Exceptional Customer Experience

Providing an exceptional customer experience is crucial for attracting and retaining customers. When customers have positive interactions with your business, they are more likely to become loyal advocates and recommend your products or services to others. Therefore, investing in customer experience can significantly contribute to attracting new customers.

Start by ensuring that your products or services meet or exceed customer expectations. Consistently deliver high-quality offerings that provide value and solve customer problems. Pay attention to product design, features, and functionality to create a positive user experience.

Additionally, focus on delivering outstanding customer service. Train your employees to be knowledgeable, friendly, and responsive to customer inquiries and concerns. Make it easy for customers to reach out to you through various channels, such as phone, email, or live chat, and strive to provide prompt and helpful resolutions.

Personalization is key in creating a memorable customer experience. Tailor your interactions and recommendations based on customer preferences and past purchase history. Use customer relationship management (CRM) tools to gather and analyze customer data, enabling you to provide personalized recommendations, offers, and communications.

Another way to enhance the customer experience is by actively seeking and valuing customer feedback. Encourage customers to provide reviews, ratings, and testimonials, and listen to their suggestions for improvement. Address any issues or complaints promptly and transparently to show that you genuinely care about their satisfaction.

Go the extra mile to surprise and delight your customers. Offer special perks, exclusive access, or personalized gestures to show your appreciation. This can create positive word-of-mouth and attract new customers through referrals.

By consistently providing an exceptional customer experience, you can build a loyal customer base and attract new customers through positive reviews and recommendations. A customer-centric approach sets your business apart from competitors and establishes a strong reputation that helps attract customers in the long run.

Step 5
Foster Relationships and Engage with Customers

Building strong relationships with customers is a crucial step in attracting and retaining their loyalty. By fostering connections and engaging with customers, you can create a sense of community and cultivate brand advocates who not only continue to support your business but also attract new customers through positive word-of-mouth.

Start by actively engaging with customers through various channels. Utilize social media platforms, online forums, and community groups to interact with your audience, respond to their comments, and address their inquiries. Encourage two-way communication by asking for feedback, opinions, and suggestions. Engaging in conversations and demonstrating genuine interest in your customers builds trust and loyalty.

Additionally, consider implementing a customer loyalty program. Reward loyal customers with exclusive benefits, discounts, or early access to new products or services. This not only incentivizes repeat business but also makes customers feel valued and appreciated.

Another effective strategy is to leverage user-generated content (UGC). Encourage customers to share their experiences, testimonials, and photos related to your products or services. This user-generated content can be shared on your website or social media platforms, showcasing real customer experiences and attracting new customers who relate to those positive stories.

Furthermore, consider hosting events or webinars to bring your customers together. These events provide opportunities for networking, knowledge sharing, and building deeper connections. They also allow you to showcase your expertise, educate your customers, and create a memorable experience that resonates with attendees.

Finally, always strive for continuous improvement based on customer feedback. Actively listen to customer suggestions and implement changes or enhancements accordingly. This demonstrates that you value their opinions and are committed to delivering an exceptional experience.

By fostering relationships and engaging with customers, you

create a loyal customer base that not only continues to support your business but also becomes advocates who attract new customers. Building a strong community around your brand fosters a positive reputation and increases the likelihood of attracting customers who resonate with your values and offerings.

CONCLUSION

attracting customers is a multi-faceted process that requires a strategic approach and continuous effort. By defining your target audience and developing a compelling unique selling proposition, you can effectively tailor your marketing efforts to reach the right people with the right message. Enhancing your online presence through an optimized website, social media engagement, and digital marketing strategies helps increase visibility and credibility.

Implementing targeted marketing campaigns and offering incentives can entice customers to choose your business over competitors. Providing exceptional customer experiences, fostering relationships, and actively engaging with customers create loyalty and generate positive word-of-mouth. By consistently refining your strategies based on customer feedback and market trends, you can continuously attract new customers and build lasting relationships. Remember, attracting customers is not a one-time task but an ongoing process that requires adaptability, customer-centricity, and a commitment to delivering value. With the right strategies and a customer-focused mindset, you can successfully attract customers and position your business for long-term growth and success.